Ms June Pass
54 5721 213A St
Langley BC V2Y 2N2

FEATURING THE ARTWORK

OF

THOMAS KINKADE

Mealtime Memories

Sharing the Warmth of Family Traditions

Publishers Since 1798

THOMAS NELSON PUBLISHERS®
a division of Thomas Nelson, Inc.
Nashville

www.ThomasNelson.com

Published in Nashville, Tennessee, by Thomas Nelson, Inc.
Scripture references are from the following sources:

Scripture quotations noted NCV are from the NEW CENTURY VERSION.
Copyright © 1987, 1988, 1991 by W Publishing, Nashville, Tennessee. Used by permission.

Scripture quotations noted NIV are taken from the HOLY BIBLE, NEW INTERNATIONAL VERSION ®. Copyright © 1973, 1978, 1984 by International Bible Society. Used by permission of Zondervan Bible Publishing House. All rights reserved.

The "NIV" and "New International Version" trademarks are registered in the United States Patent and Trademark Office by International Bible Society. Use of either trademark requires the permission of International Bible Society.

Scripture quotations marked "NKJV" are taken from the New King James Version®. Copyright © 1982 by Thomas Nelson, Inc. Used by permission. All rights reserved.

Written by The Livingstone Corporation. Project staff includes Katie E. Gieser, Paige Drygas, Mary Ann Lackland, Elisabeth Haley, Alice Dickerson, Mary E. Geiser, and Margaret A. Haley. Devotions written by Mary Ann Lackland. Recipes reviewed by Mary E. Gieser

Design and production by: Que-Net Media™, Chicago

Library of Congress Cataloging-in-Publication Data

Mealtime memories : sharing the warmth of family traditions / featuring the artwork of Thomas Kinkade. p. cm.

ISBN 0-7852-6495-7
1. Grace at meals--Christianity. 2. Cookery. I. Kinkade, Thomas, 1958-   . II. Thomas Nelson Publishers.
BV283.G7M387 2002
249--dc21

2002007722
Printed in the United States of America
02 03 04 05 06 QWV 7 6 5 4 3 2 1

Contents

Have you ever wondered why God made food so good? Why did He bother giving us taste buds to savor different sensations, and noses that distinguish certain scents from others?

I believe He made food good because He is good. And as a good God, He longs to lavish on us, His children, good things. Sometimes I think He may have given me an extra dose of that goodness, considering the degree to which I really appreciate a hearty meal. And Nanette will tell you, keeping my appetite for the right kinds of foods in check is an ongoing and often arduous ordeal. But between the two of us, we manage a blended menu of the frivolous and functional, and we have an awful lot of fun eating it together as a family.

In fact, that's what Mealtime Memories is all about—families, fellowship, and fun as it happens around the kitchen table all year long. When you think about it, food does play a pretty important role in our lives. Like clockwork, you can count on breakfast, lunch, and dinner (or at least some semblance of each) every day of your life. Why not turn those predictable moments into lifelong lasting memories? It just requires a little time, a little forethought, and a love for those sitting around the table with you.

Every season, and every month in those seasons, brings a special opportunity for you to share and experience with your family and friends. Whether it's the warmth of a wintertime stew, the cool refreshment of a summer cucumber salad, or the intimate experience of a well-planned Valentine dinner, you can bring your loved ones closer to you through this fantastic vehicle of food that God provides just for us.

In the following pages, you'll discover recipes that ring in each month and season in a distinctive and memorable way. In addition to tantalizing tastes for your tongue, you'll also discover food for the soul, with devotions, prayers, quotes and family exercises designed to take your meal experience together deeper than ever before. It is my prayer that as you sit down and look over this book, you will begin to gain the sense of community God intends for His people and gather ideas on how to create that kind of environment in your own home. Use the artwork to connect with your spouse and children on a more emotional level, allowing them to communicate their thoughts, fears, hopes, and feelings in a nurturing and supportive atmosphere. The devotionals and questions are designed to spark discussion, and hopefully new discoveries into each other's personalities, plans for the future, and personal relationships with the Lord.

Being in the kitchen, cooking up memories. Gathering around the table, connecting with others in love. It is the picture of hope God holds for His families, His intended purpose for putting us together in the first place. Let us work diligently to protect and promote the gift of life He gives us. Let us take time to stop the distractions and pull together more closely than before. Encourage each other in the Lord. Bolster one another's faith, and develop lasting friendships to take you through the years. True, time and effort are always an investment. But like the anticipation of a well-cooked meal, the bounty of blessings you experience in the end is always worth the work.

Cozy Winter Dinner

Lord, behold our family here assembled. We thank you for this place in which we dwell, for the love that unites us, for the peace accorded us this day, for the hope with which we expect the morrow; for the health, the work, the food, and the bright skies that make our lives delightful; for our friends in all parts of the earth.

Bless us, if it may be, in all our innocent endeavors; if it may not, give us the strength to endure that which is to come that we may be brave in peril, constant in tribulation, temperate in wrath, and in all changes of fortune, and down to the gates of death, loyal and loving to one another.

As the clay to the potter, as the windmill to the wind, as children of their sire, we beseech of you this help and mercy for Christ's sake.

Robert Louis Stevenson

BEEF STEW FOR THE SOUL

Pile it on, I say. The heartier the stew—the more carrots, beef, broth—the better. It has been a favorite meal of mine since childhood, much to my brother's chagrin who pled for other wintertime options. Mealtimes for us growing up were critical times of growth, though we may not have recognized it as such back then.

As a single parent, Mom went out of her way to establish a sense of normalcy, continuity, and togetherness—a task most easily achieved through sit-down meals together. No matter how hectic the week might have been, we always managed a "formal" meal together on Sundays where we would swap stories and keep a running dialogue of what was going on in each other's lives. Mom was the champion encourager, and used these golden moments to inspire, praise, and promote our goals and dreams. Aware of my passion for painting, she even hung pictures from famous artists around the room where we dined, placing my artwork right alongside.

In *Skater's Pond*, I tried to depict the sense of family I felt around that dinner table. The camaraderie, the bonding of parent to child and sibling to sibling is so important—and so easily missed—if we fail to set aside time together to enjoy each other and the good things life brings us. It can be through an adventure like skating, a family walk in the woods, or an evening spent in front of a warm fire's glow with a good cup of stew and endless time to talk. These are the treasures that last a lifetime—the pleasures of the season that stay with you forever.

Haley's Irish Stew

2 pounds beef stew meat, cut into small pieces

4 cans condensed cream of chicken soup, undiluted

4 medium carrots, cut up

2 celery stalks, cut up

2 cans white potatoes, cut up; reserve liquid

Put meat, soup, carrots, and celery stalks in crock pot; add no water or seasonings. Cook on low 8-10 hours or high 5-6 hours. Then add potatoes and a little of the liquid if the stew seems too thick. Continue to heat just long enough to warm the potatoes (a few minutes), and then serve.

Harvest Yeast Rolls

1 (1/4 ounce) package dry yeast

1/2 cup warm water (105-115 degrees)

1/4 cup sugar

1 tablespoon oil or shortening

1 teaspoon salt

1/2 cup hot water

1 egg

3 cups flour

Mix yeast and warm water in small bowl, then set aside. Mix together sugar and oil or shortening in large mixing bowl. Add salt, hot water, and egg. Then add yeast mixture and mix well. Mix in flour. Dampen a towel and cover the bowl. Let rise until double in size. Stir down, cover, and put in the refrigerator until ready for use. Or, divide into muffin pans and allow to rise again until double in size. (To make three part rolls, put three equally-sized small balls of dough in each muffin cup). Bake at 350° until done, about 8-10 minutes.

Toffee Apple Dip

1 (8 ounces) package cream cheese, softened

1/2 cup brown sugar

1/4 cup sugar

1 teaspoon vanilla

1 (8 ounces) package English toffee bits

6 apples, sliced

Mix dip ingredients, and serve with apples.

Texas Sheet Cake

2 cups sugar	1/2 cup buttermilk
2 cups flour	2 eggs
1 cup butter	1 teaspoon baking soda
1/4 cup cocoa	1 teaspoon vanilla
	1 cup water

Preheat oven to 375°. Combine sugar and flour in mixing bowl. Set aside. In a pan, bring to a simmer butter, cocoa and water and mix well. Pour over dry mixture, and mix well. Add buttermilk, eggs, baking soda, and vanilla. Spread in a greased jellyroll pan. Bake at 375° for 20 minutes.

— Icing —

1/2 cup butter, softened	3-3/4 cups (1 pound) powdered sugar
1/4 cup cocoa	1 teaspoon vanilla
1/3 cup milk	1 cup chopped pecans, optional

Beat together the icing ingredients, and frost cake once it is cooled.

Family Recipe

Like a master chef, God blends unique personalities and characters together in a flavorful creation He calls "family." One look around the dinner table at the individuals gathered together is evidence enough of His creative blend. One member of our family may be especially sweet—like a grandmother who lives to dote on her grandkids. Another member may bring a bold taste to the brew—a strong-willed sibling who is always out in front. Regardless of the combination, each ingredient is essential to the formula's success. The family setting simmers individual flavors together in order to make us who we could never otherwise be on our own. In the same way, a cook knows a successful dish does not rely on one delicious ingredient alone. We rely on each other to round out the family recipe.

Family Time

If each member of your family were a unique ingredient, how would you describe his or her role in the family recipe? For example, "Mom is like the salt in the family—she really spices things up with her fun-loving personality."

Why do you think God designed individual family members to come together like a recipe? What do you think He is cooking up with your family recipe?

Dear God,

Just one look around the table reminds us that You've made each of us so unique. Thank You for making all of us special in our own ways. Thank You even more for cooking up the idea of family so You could bring us together in love. Amen.

Our Family Traditions

Valentine's Day Dinner

O Divine Master
Grant that I may not so much seek to be consoled as to console;
To be understood as to understand;
To be loved as to love.
For it is in giving that we receive;
It is in pardoning that we are pardoned;
And it is in dying that we are born to eternal life.

Francis of Assisi

A GARDEN OF LOVE

A beautiful rose garden grew along the white picket fence of our home in Placerville. The lush beauty of the flowers against the quaint, white fence married a sense of peace and comfort in my mind every time I looked at it. Mom must have seen the beauty, too, because she carefully cultivated the garden, cutting fresh blooms to illuminate the inside of our home with their charm. It's easy to see why the rose has stood through time as the quintessential symbol of love, beauty, life and hope.

It's also understandable while my fascination with this fragile but powerful feature of God's creation stands strong, today. Now living next door to me, Mom still busies herself in her garden, growing more and more lovely roses. But I'm the one who takes joy in cutting them now—this time bringing them inside our home to my wife and family to share with them the joy they bring me. In *A Perfect Red Rose*, I even crushed some of the petals from the garden to mix in the paint, capturing its truest essence.

Our family is always looking for fun, new ways to express our love. Nanette puts notes in our girls' lunch boxes. Our girls hide letters on the refrigerator and other places in the kitchen for their mom to find while she's busy making meals. I'll find them on my easel, or waiting for me when I come home. Like a rose, it is a simple yet very tangible way to demonstrate just how precious our relationships are.

Chicken Wellington

6 boneless skinless
chicken breast halves

6 frozen pastry shells, thawed

Roll each thawed pastry shell with rolling pin until elongated enough to wrap
around breast. Wrap around breast half with ends underneath. Refrigerate
until ready to bake. Then, bake at 325° for an hour.

— Sauce —

1 (4 ounce) can mushrooms, drained

1 teaspoon butter

2 tablespoons diced fresh or
2 teaspoons dehydrated onion

1 can condensed
cream of chicken soup

2 teaspoons water

1/4 teaspoon Beau Monde (an herb blend)

Sauté mushrooms in butter. Add onions. Mix in soup, water and seasoning.
Heat through and serve over chicken.

Shaker Carrots

6–8 carrots, peeled and cut lengthwise

2 tablespoons horseradish

2 tablespoons grated onion

1/2 teaspoon salt

1/4 teaspoon pepper

1/2 cup mayonnaise

1/4 cup fine bread or cracker crumbs

1 tablespoon melted butter

dash of paprika

Put carrots in a pot with enough water to cover. Bring to a boil and cook until tender, about 15 minutes. Reserve 1 cup of the cooking liquid and discard the rest. Arrange the carrots in a shallow baking dish. Combine the horseradish, onion, carrot liquid, salt, pepper and mayonnaise. Pour over carrots. Combine the crumbs, butter and paprika; sprinkle over the top. Bake at 375° for 15-20 minutes.

Strawberry Pretzel Salad

2 cups coarsely crushed pretzels

3/4 cup margarine, melted

3 tablespoons sugar

1 (8 ounce) package cream cheese, softened

1 cup sugar

1 (8 ounce) frozen whipped topping, thawed

1 (6 ounce) strawberry gelatin

2 cups boiling water

2 (10 ounces) frozen strawberries, thawed and undrained

Mix together pretzels, margarine, and 3 tablespoons sugar. Pat into bottom of 9" x 13" pan and bake 350° for 10 minutes. Let cool. Mix cream cheese and 1 cup sugar. Fold in whipped topping. Spread over the crust and refrigerate. Dissolve gelatin in boiling water. Add strawberries. Refrigerate if necessary until slightly thickened. Pour over cream cheese mixture. Refrigerate for several hours before serving.

Red Velvet Cake

1/2 cup shortening	1 teaspoon vanilla
1 1/2 cup sugar	2 (1 ounce) bottles red food coloring
2 eggs	1 cup buttermilk
2 tablespoons cocoa	2-1/2 cups flour
1 teaspoon salt	1 tablespoon vinegar

1-1/2 teaspoons soda

In a mixing bowl, cream shortening and sugar. Beat in eggs. Add cocoa, salt, vanilla, and food coloring, mixing well. Then beat in buttermilk and flour. Add the vinegar, then baking soda. Bake at 350° for 25- 30 minutes in two greased and floured 8" or 9" round pans.

— Frosting —

5 tablespoons flour	1 cup butter, softened
1 cup milk	1 cup sugar

1 teaspoon vanilla

Cook flour and milk until thick, stirring constantly. Allow to cool, covering top of mixture with plastic wrap (to avoid a "skin" on the surface). Cream butter, sugar and vanilla in mixing bowl. Add flour and milk mixture. Beat until smooth, being careful not to over-beat. Frost the layer cake.

Love Language

Some families are huggers. Their typical greeting involves scooping each other up in bear hugs at the beginning or end of a day. Some moms are infamous note writers, slipping them into sack lunches and tucking them away into her children's luggage at summer camp. Still other families express love other ways. A dad who struggles to say the words "I love you" may show it instead by staying up all night trying to assemble a child's Christmas present. Some siblings who would rather gag than hug each other may opt for trading their favorite clothes instead. It doesn't matter how our family demonstrates love as long as we show it— consistently and often. Families have their own language to express love from the heart. Listen and look for the many ways the members of your family might say "I love you" today.

Family Time

How does your family most often demonstrate love for each other? For example, who in your family is more likely to show their love by saying kind words? Offering to do favors? Touching and hugging? Buying thoughtful gifts?

How do we know when someone loves us "from the heart"? What's the difference between liking our family and loving them at all costs?

Dear Heavenly Father,

You showed us what it means to love deeply, from the heart. We heard You say, "I love you," loud and clear when You sent Your Son to die for us on the cross. Open our ears and our eyes to the ways we can show how much we love our family today and every day. Amen.

Our Family Traditions

Easter Luncheon

O God! I bless you for the wondrous revelation of yourself in Christ crucified, the wisdom of God, and the power of God. I bless you, that while man's wisdom leaves him helpless in presence of the power of sin and death, Christ crucified proves that he is the wisdom of God by the mighty redemption he works as the power of God. And I bless you, that what he wrought and bestows as an almighty Saviour is revealed within us by the divine light of your own Holy Spirit.

Andrew Murray

There is beauty in every season, and I have an appreciation for them all. What a beautiful picture God paints for His children every spring. Each blossom, each leaf, each new birth shows the incredible resurrection power of God that we find in Christ, His Son. From the very beginning, God has been in the business of creating life out of nothing. It is no surprise, then, that He found a way to conquer the death of sin we brought on ourselves. Just like the seeds that fall in autumn, die in winter, and suddenly spring to new life in spring, so are our lives under the provision of atonement Christ makes for us on the cross. Not only did He die in our place—He rose again from the dead, demonstrating the power and place of God, and our place of life alongside Him.

Every spring, and consequently every Easter, my thoughts turn to the incredible love of God that would make such an ultimate sacrifice for an unworthy people. Like the revived trees and flowers, my soul is nourished by His presence, and awakens my heart to deeper gratitude than the year before.

Long Lake Ham Sauce

3 egg yolks

1/2 cup sugar

1 cup condensed tomato soup (undiluted)

1/2 cup prepared mustard

1/2 cup vinegar

1/2 cup soft (tub) margarine

Purée all ingredients in blender or food processor.
Brush on ham, and bake as directed.

Traditional Hash Brown Casserole

1 (2 pounds) package frozen hash browns

1 cup chopped onion

2 cups (8 ounces) shredded cheddar cheese

1 teaspoon salt

2 cans condensed cream of chicken soup

2 cups (1 pint) sour cream

1 cup corn flake crumbs

2 tablespoons margarine, melted

Mix all ingredients together except corn flake crumbs and margarine. Put into a greased 9" x 13" casserole dish. Mix the corn flake crumbs and melted margarine together and sprinkle on top. Bake at 325° for 1 hour and 15 minutes, uncovered.

To make ahead: prepare recipe as given, but do not bake. Cover and refrigerate until needed. Then, uncover and bake as directed.

Grandma's Green Beans

1 teaspoon sugar

1 tablespoon oil

1 tablespoon chopped onion

1 (15 ounce) can green beans, Italian style (flat), undrained

Combine all ingredients. Cover and cook over low heat for several hours, stirring occasionally. Estimate 2-3 servings per can of beans. For a large group, cook for at least 4 hours.

Triple Berry Trifle

1 prepared angel food cake, cubed

2 (16 ounce) packages frozen mixed berries

2 tablespoon praline liqueur (optional)

1 (5 ounces) package instant vanilla pudding

1/2 cup milk

1 (14 ounces) can sweetened condensed milk

1 (8 ounces) frozen whipped topping, thawed

Place cake in bottom of a large glass serving bowl. Distribute berries on top of cake cubes. Sprinkle with liqueur. Combine pudding, milk, sweetened condensed milk, and 1 cup whipped topping; stir well. Pour over frozen berries. Top custard with remaining whipped topping. Let sit in the refrigerator for 4 hours, enough for berries to thaw before serving.

> Therefore, if anyone is in Christ, he is a new creation; old things have passed away; behold, all things have become new.
>
> 2 CORINTHIANS 5:17 (NKJV)

New Creations

Whew! When God forgives an offense, it is as if a huge load lifts from our slumped shoulders. Guilt? Gone! Shame? Erased! Easter reminds us it's a new day because God has forgiven us. So, why do we keep that wonderful feeling of being forgiven from others in our family? Instead of setting our offender free, we often let the guilty party linger in shame. We tend to punish those we love when they hurt us . . . far more than we ourselves would want to endure. Yet the Bible tells us in effect to trip the lock, hand over the keys, and set the prisoner free. Christ has put all our offenses behind Him— we must also be willing to do the same for others. This is the meaning of Easter. We allow our family to be the new creations they are in Christ by not holding their old sins against them.

Family Time

Take turns sharing your hot buttons—the little things everyone knows set you off. What happens when people in your family push your buttons?

What does it feel like to be forgiven?
What does it feel like
to forgive someone?

Dear Jesus,

Sometimes it's just plain hard to forgive—especially when it comes to family. We want to return hurt with more hurt. Help us to leave our old ways behind us. Today, show us the meaning of Easter and how everything—every relationship— can be made new. Amen.

Our Family Traditions

Bed and Breakfast

I arise today
Through a mighty strength:
God's power to guide me,
God's might to uphold me,
God's wisdom to teach me,
God's eyes to watch over me,
God's ear to hear me,
God's Word to give me speech,
God's hand to guard me,
God's way to lie before me,
God's shield to shelter me,
God's host to secure me:
Against the snares of devils,
Against the seductions of vices,
Against everyone who shall wish me ill,
Whether far or near, many or few.

Patrick of Ireland

Sometimes I can smell it even before I get out of bed (albeit on some of my more relaxed mornings when I can sleep late). Nanette knows my passion for pancakes and waffles, and trooper that she is, she will get up early to prepare a hearty breakfast for me and the kids. Not only do I reap the benefit of her incredible culinary skills, but she makes it a fun experience for us all, shaping the pancakes into hearts or spiders or whatever her imagination cooks up, topping her creations with raisin eyes, whipped cream hair or bacon smile. Breakfast becomes a fun adventure, and we all look forward to the special treat.

More than just food, though, we anticipate each other. There is simply no better way to start the day than with Nanette and the girls. It is the moment of calm before the storm, the wind in my sails before I hit the rough seas of the day. In the blessing before the meal, we are able to give our day to God, individually and collectively as a family. We acknowledge His goodness, His faithfulness, and His integral part of our family gathering. It draws us to Him and to each other, and becomes a cornerstone of faith for me, Nanette and the girls as we all go our separate ways. Then, as we enjoy the meal, we've made a memory of faith and fun that we pray will stay with our children until they make these moments with families of their own.

Country Breakfast Casserole

1 pound pork sausage, browned

1 (8 ounce) tube crescent rolls

2 cups (8 ounces) mozzarella cheese, shredded

4 eggs, beaten

3/4 cup milk

Brown the sausage, drain. Line the bottom of a buttered 9" x 13" pan with crescent rolls—seal seams. Layer sausage and cheese over the rolls. Combine eggs and milk; pour over all. Bake at 400° for about 15 minutes. Cut into squares.

Sour Cream Streusel Coffeecake

2 cups flour

1 teaspoon baking soda

1 teaspoon baking powder

1/2 teaspoon salt

1 cup margarine, softened

1 cup sugar

1 cup (8 ounces) sour cream

1 teaspoon vanilla

1 cup chopped pecans

1/2 cup sugar

1/3 cup brown sugar

1 teaspoon cinnamon

2 eggs

Mix flour, baking soda, baking powder, and salt. In another bowl, mix margarine, sugar, eggs, sour cream, and vanilla. Add to dry ingredients. Put half of mixture in greased 9" x 13" pan. Mix together topping: pecans, 1/2 cup sugar, brown sugar, and cinnamon. Sprinkle half of the topping mixture over batter in pan. Add the other half of the dough. Sprinkle the rest of the topping. Bake at 350° for 30 minutes.

Sunrise Peach Slush Drink

1 (16 ounce) package frozen unsweetened peaches, thawed slightly; undrained

1 (12 ounce) can peach or apricot nectar

1 (6 ounce) can frozen orange juice concentrate, thawed

Peach wine cooler, chilled, or lemon-lime carbonated beverage,
chilled (7-Up works well)

In blender combine undrained peaches, nectar, and concentrate.
Cover; blend till smooth. Pour into ice-cube trays.
Cover; freeze 3-4 hours or until firm. Makes 28 cubes.
To serve, remove frozen cubes from the freezer trays,
and place 2-3 cubes in each beverage glass. Let stand 20 to 30 minutes
to thaw slightly. Add 3/4 cup wine cooler or carbonated beverage;
stir gently to make a slush.

Fruit Yogurt

1 apple, peeled, chopped

1 orange, peeled, sectioned

1/2 cup seedless grapes, halved

1 nectarine, pitted, chopped

1/2 cup strawberries

1/4 cup fresh orange juice

Plain low-fat yogurt

Combine the apple, orange, grapes, nectarine, and strawberries in a bowl; mix well. Add the orange juice; toss to combine. Chill, covered, until serving time. Serve with yogurt. Yield: 4 servings

> Because of the Lord's great love
> we are not consumed,
> for his compassions never fail.
> They are new every morning;
> great is your faithfulness.
>
> LAMENTATIONS 3:22–23 (NIV)

Family of Faith

Tomorrow. Even if we used to sleep peacefully without worrying about the next day, we now live in a world that is wide awake with worry. The media remind us we are living in a new day, with terrorists, violence, threats and danger. At work, at home, at school, abroad—we have new concerns that we had not realized even existed. In contrast, God's Word reminds us that every day is a new day when it comes to God's compassion and faithfulness. In Him, we have optimistic opportunities and possibilities that did not exist for us yesterday. When we face each new day, we can either live in fear, wondering what the day has in store for us, or we can hear the message of hope that every morning brings our way: new day; same God.

Family Time

What are some things you fear the most about the future? Make a list together as each of you reveals your top two or three fears.

How will your family respond to fear? Spend some time talking about your answer. One by one, have each person read aloud an item from the "Family Fears" list you have created. After reading each fear, have the family confidently repeat the verse above: "Great is your faithfulness." Cross through each fear on the list each time you repeat this verse.

Dear God,

So many things frighten us about the future. Yet the sun came up today, didn't it? You are still in control, watching over us each day. This morning, show us how to be a family of faith, not a family of fear. Amen.

Our Family Traditions

English Tea for Mother's Day

O Lord God, whose will it is that, next to yourself, we should hold our parents in highest honor; it is not the least of our duties to beseech your goodness towards them. Preserve, I pray, my parents and home, in the love of your religion and in health of body and mind. Grant that through me no sorrow may befall them; and finally, as they are kind to me, so may you be to them, O supreme Father of all.

Desiderius Erasmus

INVISIBLE GLUE

She didn't have much. No outside support. No husband to help her through. And three kids, to boot. My mom is an amazing woman. And I was as impressed with her growing up as I still am today. She had the remarkable ability to take very little and turn it into abundance, constantly providing us with opportunities to help us learn, grow, and mostly feel special. Because of her continual efforts to expose us to all the good experiences life has to offer, I was able to see the loving hand of a Heavenly Father, even though my earthly father had left our family long before.

Needless to say, I look forward to Mother's Day. It's an opportunity for me to declare my gratitude to the woman who made such a difference in my life. Following in my footsteps, my girls love to lavish Nanette with all kinds of goodies on her special day, whether it's making breakfast in bed, creating special crafts, or just crawling in her lap to tell her how much she is appreciated.

I believe that good moms are the invisible glue that holds families together. Their uncanny ability to perceive hurts and needs, and the know-how to make it better is one of God's greatest miracles. Unfortunately, their work is often so expected, so reliable, and so behind-the-scenes, that we forget (or worse, never notice at all) the silent service that keeps us from coming apart. We succeed and surge ahead, but we fail to see the secret acts of love that keep us in full sail. After Mother's Day comes and goes, continue to lift your Mom up in prayer for the strength she needs to do all the incredible things she does.

Hot Spiced Tea

1 teaspoon whole cloves

1 1-inch cinnamon stick

6 cups water

2-1/2 tablespoons black tea

3/4 cup orange juice

2 tablespoons lemon juice

1/2 cup sugar

Add spices to water. Heat to boiling. Add tea, and steep for 5 minutes. Heat fruit juices and sugar.

Cream Scones

2 cups flour

3 teaspoons baking powder

1/2 teaspoon salt

2 tablespoons sugar

1/4 cup butter

1/2 cup whipping cream

2 eggs

sugar

Stir together the flour, baking powder, salt and sugar. Cut the butter into this mixture with pastry blender or food processor. Whisk cream and eggs together and add to mixture. Pat to 3/4-inch thickness in a greased 9" x 13" pan. Sprinkle with sugar. Bake at 375° until lightly browned, about 20 minutes. Cut and serve while hot. Yield: 1 dozen.

Lemon Curd

1 cup sugar

3 large eggs

1 egg yolk

1/2 cup (1 stick) unsalted butter, cut into pieces

6 tablespoons fresh lemon juice

2 tablespoons grated lemon peel

Whisk all ingredients together in a heavy, medium-sized saucepan over low heat until butter melts. Cook until mixture thickens to consistency of lightly whipped cream, whisking constantly; about 5 minutes. Cover and refrigerate until cold, about 4 hours. Can be prepared two days ahead.

Cranberry Orange Scones

2 cups flour

2 teaspoons baking powder

1/2 teaspoon baking soda

1/2 teaspoon salt

1/2 cup (1 stick) butter

1 cup dried cranberries

3 tablespoons sugar

2 teaspoons grated orange rind

3/4 cup plain yogurt or buttermilk

Mix flour, baking powder, baking soda, and salt in a large bowl.
Cut in butter with pastry blender or food processor until mixture
looks like coarse granules. Add cranberries, sugar, and orange rind;
toss lightly to distribute evenly. Add the yogurt or buttermilk to the flour mixture.
Stir with fork until soft dough forms.

Turn dough out onto lightly floured board and knead 5-6 times, just until well mixed.
Pat into a flat circle, about 3/4 inches thick. Put on a greased cookie sheet; cut dough
with a knife, making 8 wedges. Separate slightly. Bake at 400° for 15-20 minutes.

English Tea for Mother's Day

Ginger Cookies

4-1/2 cups flour

4 teaspoons ground ginger

2 teaspoons baking soda

1-1/2 teaspoons ground cinnamon

1 teaspoon ground cloves

1-1/2 cups shortening

2 cups sugar

2 eggs

1/2 cup molasses

3/4 cup sugar

1/4 teaspoon salt

In a mixing bowl stir together the flour, ginger, baking soda, cinnamon, cloves, and salt. In a large mixing bowl beat shortening until softened. Gradually add 2 cups sugar; beat until fluffy. Add eggs and molasses; beat well. Add half of flour mixture; beat until combined. Add the rest of the mixture, stirring with a wooden spoon. Shape dough into walnut-sized balls and roll in the rest of the sugar. Place on an ungreased cookie sheet and bake at 350° for 10-12 minutes or until light brown and puffed.

> *Then God saw everything that He had made, and indeed it was very good.*
>
> GENESIS 1:31 (NKJV)

God's Good Creation

God did a good thing when He created mothers. Like a sculptor putting the final touches on a masterpiece, He must have stepped back in satisfaction at the sight. Soft hands for soothing our worried brows. Long arms for wrapping around us when we need a hug. A big heart for sharing our greatest joys and deepest sorrows. Good eyesight for seeing exactly where it hurts. Mothers are made-to-order for meeting our needs. This Mother's Day, for whatever reason, your family may not be able to celebrate with mom in the way you would like. However, you can still celebrate your mom. Celebrate the woman God put in your life to fulfill that crucial role. Remember, she is God's good creation.

Family Time

Why do you think God did a good thing when He created mothers? When it comes to mothers, what physical characteristic means the most to you and why? Soft hands, long arms, a big heart, or good eyesight?

This Mother's Day, the best present you could give your mom is a reminder of your love. Take turns having each family member fill in the blank: "Mom, I really appreciate you because . . . _____."

Dear God,

You did a good thing when You created mothers. We know our family just wouldn't be the same without her. A mother's love reminds us just how much You love us. Help us to express to her today how much she means to us. Amen.

Our Family Traditions

Father's Day Dinner

Give, I pray you, to all children grace reverently to love their parents, and lovingly to obey them. Teach us all that filial duty never ends or lessens; and bless all parents in their children, and all children in their parents.

Christina Rossetti

HIS SOURCE OF STRENGTH

Despite my passion and joy in the role, being a good father and husband has not always been easy. Before I became known as the Painter of Light, it was easy to set priorities in order—and keep them that way—because the demands on my time and talents were simpler. But with each new success and each new door that God opened for my family and me, new challenges arose with it. In many ways I felt my ideals slipping—the sacred time with my loved ones that I so cherished and desired sliding away under the rush of each new responsibility.

God has shown me much as a husband and a father through these blessings and trials that have come our way. I've discovered that most men are easily confused beasts. We simply don't have the same sense of order that women often do, and we need time to sort things out to determine vision and direction. Issues get clouded, directions are befuddled, and men get discouraged. But there is hope. It's one of the reasons why I painted *It Doesn't Get Much Better*. There is strength found in occasional solitude, in escaping the daily grind to draw close to God, and to reconsider the direction we're going in life. I have found nature to be one of the most natural vehicles to take me away from the world's temptations and to set my spirit free to commune with my Creator—to get back to my roots, and to remember who and Whose I am. Nanette, my best friend, and others whom I love and trust are reliable sources of strength, perspective, and support. My children are the icing on the cake.

Nana's BBQ Ribs

6-8 pounds pork country style ribs, with bone or boneless

—BBQ sauce—

1 -1/2 cups ketchup	2 teaspoons salt
1/4 cup vinegar	2 teaspoons Worcestershire sauce
1/4 cup brown sugar	1/2 teaspoon pepper
1 teaspoon chili powder	1 teaspoon ginger
2 onions, minced	2 (12 ounce) jars apricot jam

To make BBQ sauce, combine sauce ingredients in saucepan
and simmer for 20 minutes.

Place ribs in roasting pan, fat side up, and bake at 450° for 30 minutes.
Drain. Reduce heat to 350° and bake for 30 minutes, fat side down. Drain.
Reduce heat to 300° and pour BBQ sauce over meat. Cover with foil
and bake for 1-1/2 hours, basting often.

Exploded Potato Salad

6-8 potatoes, baked and chopped

1 pound bacon, cooked and chopped

1 bunch green onions, sliced

1 bottle (16 ounce) ranch dressing

4 cups (1 pound) sharp cheddar cheese, shredded

1 bunch fresh parsley, chopped

Mix all ingredients, put into a 9" x 13" baking dish.
Bake at 350° for 20-25 minutes. Serve warm or cold.

Corkscrew Swamp Spoonbread

2 (8-1/2 ounce) packages corn muffin mix

1/2 cup oil

1 (17 ounce) can cream style corn

1 onion, chopped

1 clove garlic, crushed

3 eggs

1 cup buttermilk

1 cup (4 ounce) shredded cheddar cheese

Mix all ingredients together. Put into a greased 9" x 13" pan.
Bake at 350° for 45 minutes.

Buster Bar Dessert

40 chocolate sandwich cookies, crushed

1/2 cup margarine, melted

1/2 gallon vanilla ice cream, slightly softened

1 (16 ounce) jar hot fudge topping

1 (12 ounce) can Spanish peanuts

Combine cookies and margarine; press into a 9" x 13" pan. Cut ice cream into 1-inch slices and lay on top of cookie base. Spread hot fudge topping over ice cream. Sprinkle with peanuts. Cover and freeze for several hours or overnight.

The Command with a Promise

It's not always easy being the one in charge. Believe it or not, fathers need to be reassured in their role as leader. Sometimes the fathers with the toughest exteriors have the softest hearts inside. Behind his double-breasted business suit or everyday working shirt is a man learning to lead a family. Remember, they have never done this before. They may never say it, but fathers need reminders of how their family feels about them. Reminders like "we love you," "we need you," "we trust you." Families who make a point to honor the role of fathers flourish where others flounder. This command is not about children putting parents on a power trip. It's really not about parents at all. It's about God. We honor Him by honoring our parents. In return, God promises His best blessings. It's a deal that no family can refuse.

Family Time

Why do you think it is hard to be a father?

*This Father's Day, the best present you could give
your dad is a reminder of your love. Take turns
having each family member fill in the blank:
"Dad, I really appreciate you because . . .*
_____."

Dear God,

*Our family has good reason to obey Your Word. You promise
to give us Your best when we give our father our best.
We honor You today as we celebrate Father's Day. Thank You
for fathers who lead the way for us. Amen.*

Our Family Traditions

Independence Day Family Picnic

Almighty God, we make our earnest prayer that you will keep the United States in your holy protection; that you will incline the hearts of the citizens to cultivate a spirit of subordination and obedience to government, and entertain a brotherly affection and love for one another and for their fellow citizens of the United States at large. And, finally, that you will most graciously be pleased to dispose us all to do justice, to love mercy, and to demean ourselves with that charity, humility, and pacific temper of mind which were the characteristics of the Divine Author of our blessed religion and without which we can never be a happy nation. Grant our supplications, we beseech you, through Jesus Christ our Lord. Amen.

George Washington

RIGHT ROOTS

As far back as I can remember, 4th of July celebrations meant three things: patriotism, people, and pigging out. Being such a small town, Placerville didn't have much to boast. But come July 4th, we'd pull out all the stops and celebrate the day with festivities and fireworks at Rotary Park, the main meeting place for Little League games and every other get-together that would happen all year long. Mom would pack the traditional 4th of July picnic, complete with ice cream, and sparklers to round out the day.

But my father was the real inspiration behind my love of history. Often, we'd spend the 4th with his friends in Sacramento, learning about his life there. As a World War II veteran, and a member of the VFW and American Legion, he had lots of stories to tell. Enraptured by his adventures and sacrifice, I came to understand the importance of freedom and the fierce price others paid so I could enjoy it. I've never had to face the harsh reality of war. But I do want to pass on to my children the values for which our forefathers fought. I want them to know that freedom is never free, and we must never take our inalienable rights for granted.

I painted *The Light of Freedom* in response to events on September 11. The flag captures for me the spirit of America, the determined independence and freedom as given to us by God and under God. It waves as a banner of hope, a symbol of unity amid a diverse and dynamic nation. May God continue our growth, as individuals and together as a people, to replace pride and self-reliance with a dependence upon Him, and rediscover what our forefathers knew as the only root of hope—God Himself.

Summer Chicken Marinade

1/2 cup olive oil

1/2 cup brown sugar

1/2 cup soy sauce

1/2 cup sherry

6 pounds chicken parts

Mix olive oil, brown sugar, soy sauce, and sherry. Pierce the chicken with a fork to allow for more absorption of marinade. Place chicken in a heavy, self-closing plastic bag. Add marinade and coat chicken evenly. Seal and refrigerate 8-12 hours. Cook on grill, broil, or bake at 350° for 45 minutes.

Strawberry Spinach Salad

2 tablespoons sesame seeds

1/2 sugar

1 tablespoon minced onion

1/4 teaspoon Worcestershire sauce

1/4 teaspoon paprika

1/4 cup cider vinegar

1/2 cup vegetable oil

1 tablespoon poppy seeds

1 pound fresh spinach, washed, trimmed and chilled

1 quart fresh strawberries, hulled and sliced

Toast sesame seeds in a pie plate in a 350° oven for 10-12 minutes or until golden. Mix sugar, onion, Worcestershire, paprika, and vinegar in blender. Slowly add vegetable oil. Stir in sesame and poppy seeds. Chill dressing. Combine spinach and dressing right before serving. Gently toss in strawberries.

Independence Day Family Picnic

Butterscotch Sticky Rolls

18 frozen dinner rolls (unbaked dough)

1/2 cup butter, melted

1 (4 ounce) package dry butterscotch pudding mix (not instant)

3/4 cup brown sugar

3/4 teaspoon cinnamon

1/2 cup pecans, coarsely chopped

Place frozen rolls in bottom of greased bundt, angel food,
or 9" x 13" pan. Pour 1/4 cup melted butter over rolls.
Combine pudding mix, brown sugar, and cinnamon; sprinkle half
of this mixture over the rolls. Pour remaining butter over rolls;
sprinkle remaining mixture over the butter. Sprinkle with pecans.
Let rolls rise for about 8-12 hours at room temperature, uncovered.
Bake at 350° for 15-20 minutes or until deep golden brown.
Invert onto serving platter.

This recipe is also ideal for breakfast or brunch.

Fresh Fruit Pizza

1 (17 ounces) package sugar cookie mix or refrigerated tube
of sugar cookie dough

1 (8 ounces) package cream cheese, softened

1 cup powdered sugar

1 cup sugar

3 tablespoons cornstarch

1 cup water

3 tablespoons strawberry gelatin

Fruit (kiwi, strawberries, blueberries, pineapple, mandarin oranges, etc.)

Prepare cookie mix as directed on package. Lightly grease a 12" pizza pan; press
dough into pan and bake at 350° for 8-10 minutes. Cool. Whip cream cheese and
powdered sugar. Spread on cooled crust. In small saucepan, combine sugar,
cornstarch and water. Cook over medium heat until thick and clear, stirring
constantly. Stir in dry gelatin. Remove from heat and cool. Spread over cream
cheese. Arrange desired fruit pieces in an attractive pattern over the glaze. Chill
in the refrigerator and cut into wedges to serve.

> Therefore if the Son
> makes you free,
> you shall be free indeed.
>
> JOHN 8:36 (NKJV)

Ultimate Freedom

We may celebrate living in a free country, which is an incredible gift, yet we are never truly free, as God intended us to be, apart from Christ. We are grateful for the many men and women who willingly paid a price so that our country could experience earthly freedom. However, only one person could pay the price for our spiritual freedom: Jesus Christ, God's own Son.

Why do so many families miss out on spiritual freedom? Greed, envy, anger, materialism, selfishness—any and all kinds of sin. However, God's Son sets our families free from sin. Earthly freedom is a privilege we receive at birth, as Americans. Spiritual freedom is something we receive at our new birth—our second, spiritual birth when we ask Christ into our lives. He paid the ultimate price for our eternal freedom. Now, that's worth celebrating!

Family Time

Who in your church, neighborhood or community helped pay the price for your earthly freedom (a veteran or current member of our armed forces)? What can your family do together this month to show your appreciation for them? (For example, make a batch of homemade cookies or a giant appreciation card, and deliver it to your local National Guard office).

What do you think spiritual freedom means to your family? What may be strangling your family's spiritual freedom (sin such as greed, anger or selfishness)? Ask God to set you free from these things.

Dear Jesus,

We seem to know more about earthly temptation than spiritual freedom. Whenever we are tempted to give in to sin and give up our freedom, please come to our rescue. Set us free, Lord, to live for You. Amen.

Our Family Traditions

Seafood Supper

I asked for strength that I might achieve;
I was made weak that I might learn humbly to obey.

I asked for health that I might do greater things;
I was given infirmity that I might do better things.

I asked for riches that I might be happy;
I was given poverty that I might be wise.

I asked for power that I might have the praise of men;
I was given weakness that I might feel the need of God.

I asked for all things that I might enjoy life;
I was given life that I might enjoy all things.

I got nothing that I had asked for,
but everything that I had hoped for.

Almost despite myself my unspoken prayers were answered;
I am, among all men, most richly blessed.

An Unknown Confederate Soldier

When I painted *Perseverance*, from the Life Values Collection, the promise of reward received by pressing on loomed large in my view. God never tells us in His Word that we will sail through life without any storms, that Christians will never encounter difficulties on the way. On the contrary, He warns us that trials and tribulations indeed will come, and unless we know where to cast our anchor, life's toughest tests can shake us to the hull and even tear us apart. It is critical to know how to find harbor in Him, even in the midst of life's open and raging seas. If we know how to rely on His guidance and support when life is good, then we can remember the light when the skies grow dark. Though the waves buffet and break hard against us, we can overcome the strongest assault, because our God who sends even the storm still stands by our side.

Worldly props on which we lean are worthless. The life preserver God throws out to us is prayer, the vital connection between Creator and creature that saves us from the storm and pulls us back to the Father's safety. It is in the sanctuary of communion with God that we gain the strength to surge ahead. It is here where His Spirit blows wind in our sails and sets us back on course to Him.

Shrimp Quiche Lorraine

1 pound frozen or fresh shrimp

1-1/2 cups (6 ounces) shredded cheddar cheese

1/3 cup sliced green onion

1 10-inch baked pastry shell

4 eggs

1-1/2 cups light cream

1/2 teaspoon salt

Pinch cayenne

1/4 teaspoon paprika

1/2 cup coarsely chopped pecans

Cook, shell, de-vein and dice shrimp. Sprinkle shrimp, cheese and onions over bottom of baked pastry shell. Beat eggs slightly in a medium-size bowl; beat in cream, salt, cayenne and paprika; pour over shrimp. Sprinkle with pecans. Bake at 325° for 50 minutes.

Jamie's Super Salad

Dressing

4 tablespoons sugar

1 teaspoon salt

1/4 teaspoon pepper

1/2 cup oil

2-4 tablespoons vinegar

Salad

1 head lettuce (romaine or iceberg)

6 slices bacon, cooked and crumbled

4 tablespoons sesame seeds, toasted

1/4 cup sliced almonds, toasted

4 green onions, chopped

1/2 (3 ounce) can chow mein noodles

Combine dressing ingredients, mixing well; chill. Combine salad ingredients, toss with dressing just before serving.

Lemon Sage Red Snapper

1/2 cup low-sodium chicken broth

4 (1/2-inch-thick) red snapper fillets

Celtic salt and pepper to taste

3 tablespoons fresh lime juice

3 tablespoons extra virgin olive oil

1/4 teaspoon minced scallion

1 teaspoon crumbled sage

Preheat the oven to 350 degrees. Lightly grease a shallow baking dish large enough to hold the fish in a single layer. Pour the chicken broth in the baking dish. Season the fish on both sides with salt and pepper; place in the baking dish. Drizzle the lime juice and olive oil over the fish. Sprinkle with scallion and sage. Bake for 10 to 12 minutes, basting occasionally with the pan juices. Yield: 4 servings

Adapted from a recipe found on RecipeLand.com

Strawberry Angel Pie

3 egg whites

1 cup superfine or granulated sugar

1 teaspoon vanilla or almond extract

1 (3 ounce) pkg. strawberry gelatin

1/4 teaspoon cream of tartar

1-1/4 cups boiling water

1 cup sliced fresh strawberries or 1 (10 ounce) package frozen sliced strawberries, thawed and drained

1 cup whipping cream, whipped

To prepare meringue shell: Preheat oven to 275°. Have egg whites at room temperature. Add vanilla, cream of tartar, and a dash of salt. Beat until frothy. Gradually add sugar, a little at a time, beating until very stiff peaks form and sugar is dissolved. Spoon into greased 9-inch pie plate and shape into a shell, swirling sides high. Bake at 275° for one hour. Turn off the heat and let dry in oven (door closed) at least two hours.

Dissolve gelatin in boiling water. Chill until consistency of unbeaten egg white. Fold in strawberries and whipped cream. Chill until mixture mounds slightly when spooned. Pile into meringue shell. Chill 4-6 hours or overnight. Garnish with additional whipped cream and strawberry halves, if desired.

Walking Without Fainting

Life is not a fifty-yard dash; it is a marathon. Sometimes everything seems to be going well. We feel like we are soaring through life. At other times, we are running madly from activity to activity, with hardly any time to rest. Still at other times, the best we can do is just to walk without fainting. We may be tired and worn out. As summer winds down and the new school year approaches, we may feel defeated before we even get started. At these times, it is all we can do to focus on the next step and trust we will not fall. It is during those tough times when we need to listen carefully for the still but sure voice of our Father. He cheers us onward, calling us to take one more step. As long as we keep moving, we are winning in the race of life. Soon we will run, and after that, we will soar again.

Family Time

What are you looking forward to doing this school year (i.e., extracurricular activities, playing a sport, a business trip, etc.)?

Part of what keeps us going is setting goals. When we reach one goal, we strive for the next one. What are your family goals for this school year? Set a goal for each category of your life, such as spiritual (read a daily devotion), physical (cook healthy meals twice a week), financial (eat out less), and social (host a neighborhood cookout).

Dear Father,

When we feel like we cannot take another step, help us to listen for Your voice cheering us onward. Fuel our family with Your strength this school year. Give us wisdom as we set out to meet our goals. Amen.

Our Family Traditions

A Hearty Country Farm Dinner

Give us grace, O Lord, to work while it is day, fulfilling diligently and patiently whatever duty Thou appointest us; doing small things in the day of small things, and great labors if Thou summon us to any … Go with me, and I will go; but if Thou go not with me, send me not; let me hear Thy voice when I follow. Amen.

Christina Rossetti

PERFECT PEACE

The pace quickens. The schedule is packed. As September rolls around, so all the activities that clamor for my and my family's time. And I have to say it's exciting. I love the change of season and the promise of what lies ahead for me in my career and in the new school year for the girls. But it is also easy to get caught up in the chaos. To become distracted by all the different possibilities, losing sight of the few that God has chosen for us to do.

It is important to remember that God has already ordained for us all the works He intends for us to accomplish. Our job is simply to seek out His will, and go where He leads. When I painted *Sunset at Riverbend Farm*, it was my first depiction of a working farm, an idyllic setting where even the animals seem at peace at the end of a long day's work. I believe that the serenity and peace that comes from obedience on a daily basis can be ours, as God's children.

Overstuffed Peppers

4-6 green peppers

1 pound ground beef

3 tablespoons onion, chopped

3/4 cup bread crumbs

1 egg, beaten

1/2 cup milk

2 teaspoons Worcestershire sauce

1 teaspoon salt

1/4-1/2 teaspoon Tabasco sauce

1 cup (4 ounces) shredded cheddar cheese

1 (8 ounces) can tomato sauce

Cut tops off of peppers. Brown beef; add onion and cook until tender. Drain.
Stir everything else but the cheese and tomato sauce together and add to
ground beef. Lightly stuff into the peppers. Place peppers in crock pot.
Sprinkle with cheese. Pour tomato sauce over all.
Cover and cook on low 8-10 hours or on high 4-5 hours.

Crescent Dinner Rolls

1 (1/4 ounce) packet dry yeast

1/2 cup sugar

1 cup milk, lukewarm

2 eggs, well beaten

1 teaspoon salt

1/2 cup butter, melted

4 cups flour

Mix yeast, sugar and milk in large mixing bowl. Let stand at room temperature for half an hour. Add remaining ingredients, stirring well to make a soft dough. Cover with a light cloth and leave out all night (8-10 hours), without refrigeration. Put risen dough on floured surface, punch down and divide into thirds. Roll each portion into a circle (about 10" in diameter). Cut into 8 wedges and roll up each wedge, starting from wide end.

Place on greased cookie sheets, cover with light cloth and let rise for 6 hours. Bake at 400° for 6-7 minutes.

Swedish Nut Cake

2 cups sugar

2 cups flour

1/2 teaspoon salt

2 eggs

1-1/2 teaspoon baking soda

2/3 cup chopped pecans

1 (20 ounces) can crushed pineapple, undrained

Mix all of the ingredients in a large mixing bowl by hand.
Do not use mixer. Pour into greased and floured 9" x 13" pan
and bake at 350° for 30-35 minutes.
Make icing while cake bakes.

Swedish Nut Cake

— Icing —

1 (8 ounces) cream cheese, softened

1/2 cup margarine, softened, or shortening

3-3/4 cups (1 pound) powdered sugar

Mix all ingredients together until smooth.
(Mix on high to make icing fluffy). Pour on cake while cake is hot.

To freeze cake: freeze uncovered for over an hour.
Then cover first with plastic wrap and then with aluminum foil.

> In all the work you are doing, work the best you can. Work as if you were doing it for the Lord, not for people.
>
> COLOSSIANS 3:23 (NCV)

Give and Take

We may feel like we have a give-and-take relationship with our work, our school, our friends, and even our family. We give, give, give and everyone else just takes, takes, takes. When it comes down to it, we'd really like others to appreciate us once in a while. It's easy to feel under-appreciated—especially under our own roof! Families are sometimes the worst at taking each other for granted. However, the Bible says we should continually give our best effort for God's sake, not so that others will notice. We work hard at being a good parent, a good son or daughter, or a good student in order to please God, not others. When it seems like we are doing our best without receiving any reward, remember that God notices. He sees. And He will reward us for our efforts.

Family Time

Name something each member of your family has done in the past month or so that deserves extra appreciation or applause. For example, Dad got a raise at work, a child took out the trash without being asked, Mom baked cookies for a child's sleepover, etc. Make sure to include every member of the family.

What does it mean to work at something with your whole heart? What favorite activity do you put your whole heart into and why?

Dear God,

Sometimes we feel under-appreciated in our family. Remind us to thank and encourage one another more often. Even more so, help us do our best to help the family, for Your sake—not just so that others will notice. Amen.

Our Family Traditions

Campfire Supper

We must praise your goodness that you have left nothing undone to draw us to yourself. But one thing we ask of you, our God, not to cease to work in our improvement. Let us tend towards you, no matter by what means, and be fruitful in good works, for the sake of Jesus Christ our Lord.

Ludwig van Beethoven

COOL CHANGE

Maybe it's the crackling, crunching sound I hear with every step. Or the vivid hues of amber and gold, waving among the dwindling sea of green. The distinctive scent of piled up leaves, slowly burning into oblivion. The crisp, cool autumn breeze, alerting me that times have changed. Summer is gone. And soon the harvest festivities will begin. Instead of always being on the go, I begin to crave the comforts of home. Curling up by the fire with family. Feeling the security warmth of shelter that shields me from the cold world without.

The changing seasons beckon me home—where I belong. I believe it is God's subtle way of reminding us that while we are here on this earth, nothing is permanent. Even the extravagant growth of spring, the life of summer, and the beauty of fall are fleeting. One thing remains sure, though: that God holds for us a heavenly home that will never fade away. One day we will be with Him in Paradise, enjoying a creation that does not die and fellowshipping with family that will never end.

So I see fall through the eyes of promise. Promise that there's more to come. That the grandeur of creation only begins to tell the story of hope that God holds for those who trust Him. And until that day when I will see Him face to face, I will anticipate His presence more with every hayride and pumpkin patch I see. A chill is in the air. And good times are coming. I wait for them with eager anticipation.

Bacon-Wrapped Chicken

4 (6 ounce) boneless skinless chicken breast halves

4 (1 ounce) slices cream cheese

chopped chives to taste

4 slices bacon

1 can condensed cream of chicken soup

1/2 cup mayonnaise

1/2 cup milk

1 teaspoon lemon juice

1/4 teaspoon ground black pepper

salt to taste

Pound the chicken breasts until flat. Put a slice of cream cheese and a few chopped chives in the middle of each breast and roll up. Wrap each rolled breast with 1 slice of bacon and secure with toothpicks. To make sauce: Combine the soup, mayonnaise, milk, lemon juice, pepper and salt. Mix all together until smooth. Place wrapped chicken pieces in a 9" x 13" baking dish and cover with the sauce mixture. Bake at 325° for 1 hour. Makes 4 servings.

Cheddar Bay Biscuits

2 cups biscuit mix

2/3 cup milk

1/2 cup (2 ounces) shredded cheddar cheese

1/4 cup parmesan cheese

1/4 cup butter or margarine

1/2 teaspoon garlic powder

1 teaspoon parsley flakes

Stir together biscuit mix, milk and cheeses until soft dough forms. Drop by
spoonfuls on an ungreased cookie sheet. Bake at 450° for 10-12 minutes.
Melt butter or margarine, and stir in garlic powder and parsley flakes.
Brush over warm biscuits.

Easy Creamed Spinach

2 (10 ounce) packages frozen chopped spinach, cooked

1 (1 ounce) package dry onion soup mix

2 cups (1 pint) sour cream

1/2 cup (2 ounces) shredded cheddar cheese

Grease a two quart casserole dish. Drain spinach. In a medium mixing bowl combine spinach, soup mix, and sour cream. Spoon into greased casserole dish and top with cheese. Bake at 350° about 25 minutes, or until heated through.

Fall Creek Apple Crisp

4-5 medium-sized apples

2 cups sugar

2 eggs

2 cups flour

1/2 cup butter, softened

cinnamon and sugar

Peel and slice apples, and put into a greased 9" x 13" baking dish.
Mix the sugar, eggs, flour and butter together, and cover the apples.
Sprinkle with cinnamon and sugar, and bake at 350° for 40 minutes.

Things are Looking Up

This beautiful time of year reminds us of God's majesty. The changing colors of the leaves reflect the dazzling brilliance of God's reign in heaven. Sometimes we need to take a break from focusing on everything around us here on earth, like our school schedules, deadlines, soccer practices, and homework. We need to think about what awaits us in heaven. Creation can help us do that. When we are on our commute to work or our walk to school, we need to remember to look up from the road every now and then. See the trees, smell the distinctive fall air, and feel the brisk wind beginning to blow. God created the earth and its beauty to remind us that we haven't seen anything yet. Just wait until we get to heaven! His greatness will amaze us. His majesty will astound us. When life gets us down, as it sometimes will, we need to remind ourselves to look up.

Family Time

Take a family hike sometime this month. Pick up as many different colors and shapes of leaves as you can find. Examine them closely. See the veins of color in each one. Spend some time talking about the God who created the beauty around you.

What are you most looking forward to seeing in heaven? Describe what you think it will be like.

Dear God,

It's good to look up from our daily routine and focus on You and Your majesty. Sometimes we get so caught up in our earthly lives that we forget where we are headed—heaven. Thank You for creating beauty here on earth as a reminder of what is waiting for us there in heaven. Amen.

Our Family Traditions

Traditional Thanksgiving Dinner

O My God, let me, with thanksgiving, remember, and confess unto you your mercies on me. Let my bones be bedewed with your love, and let them say unto you, who is like unto you, O Lord? You have broken my bonds in pieces. I will offer to you the sacrifice of thanksgiving. And how you have broken them, I will declare; and all who worship you, when they hear this, will say, "Blessed is the Lord, in Heaven and in earth, great and wonderful is his name."

Augustine

AN ATTITUDE OF GRATITUDE

They knew they were fortunate. Better off than most. And they were generally thankful. But Merritt and Chandler, my two oldest girls, didn't understand the depth of their privilege until they witnessed first-hand life as it is for many in third world countries. As part of a mission trip with World Vision, we toured several Guatemalan villages one summer. We lent help but received far more than we gave—for each family we met taught us life lessons that we will never forget.

Acknowledging God's grace and goodness in every detail of our lives has to characterize our lives as Christians. Not only do we enjoy the physical blessings God bestows, but we belong to an incredible God. He considers us His own. And we hold every spiritual blessing in the heavenly places as His heirs.

Thanksgiving is a natural time to reflect on God's incredible bounty. The golden brown turkey, all the trimmings, and my favorite—apple pie—bring our extended family together to the tabl,e and we stay there literally for hours.

But I want it to be even more than that. I want my family to develop an attitude of gratitude that goes beyond the day into the rest of the year. Before every meal and every exciting opportunity, to take time out to thank the Giver of all good gifts. May the memory of our mission experience motivate our hearts to value the things that God cherishes, and to happily acknowledge His loving hand as He allows us to experience them together.

Make-Ahead Mashed Potatoes

10 medium Idaho potatoes

1/2 cup butter

1 teaspoon salt

1 tablespoon grated onions

1 cup scalded milk

1 (8 ounce) brick cream cheese, softened

paprika

Heat a pot of salted water to boiling. Add potatoes and cook until tender, about 15 minutes. Drain and put potatoes in a mixing bowl. Beat with an electric mixer until smooth. Add the rest of the ingredients and mix well. Add more milk if needed. Spread potatoes into a greased 9" x 13" casserole and sprinkle with paprika. Refrigerate overnight. Take potatoes out of the refrigerator 1-1/2 hours before baking. Bake uncovered at 350° for 45 minutes.

Slow-Cooked Stuffing

1 cup butter or margarine

2 cups chopped onion

2 cups chopped celery

1/4 cup parsley sprigs

2 (8 ounce) cans mushrooms, drained

12 to 13 cups cubed seasoned stuffing mix

3-1/2 to 4-1/2 cups chicken broth or turkey broth

2 eggs, well-beaten

Melt butter in skillet and sauté onion, celery, parsley and mushrooms. Pour over stuffing mix in a very large mixing bowl. Mix together. Pour in enough broth to moisten, add beaten eggs, and mix well. Pack lightly into crock pot. Cover and set on high for 45 minutes. Reduce to low and cook for 4-8 hours.

Baked Acorn Squash

2 acorn squash

1/4 cup butter

1/2 cup brown sugar

cinnamon

salt

pepper

Cut squash in half. Place cut side down in baking dish and bake at 350° for 30 minutes. Turn right side up, and in each half place 1 tablespoon butter, 2 tablespoons brown sugar, and a sprinkling of cinnamon, salt, and pepper. Return to oven for another 30 minutes.

Peas Extraordinaire

1 pound frozen baby peas, thawed

1 (11 ounce) can cream of celery soup

1/2 cup crumbled, cooked bacon

1 (8 ounce) can water chestnuts, sliced and cut into thirds

1/4 cup chopped onion

1 cup seasoned crumbled stuffing

2 tablespoons butter, melted

1/4 cup dry sherry

Put peas into a greased 8" x 8" pan. Mix together soup, bacon, chestnuts and onions. Spoon onto peas. Sprinkle with stuffing. Drizzle with the butter and pour on the sherry. Bake at 350° for 30 minutes, uncovered.

Paige's Pumpkin Cheesecake

— Crust —

1-1/2 cups ginger snap crumbs   1/2 cup finely chopped pecans

1/2 cup butter, melted

Mix crumbs, pecans and butter. Press into 9" springform pan,
on the bottom and 1-1/2 inches up sides.
Bake at 350° for 10 minutes.

Paige's Pumpkin Cheesecake

— Filling —

2 (8 ounce) packages cream cheese
or Neufchatel cheese, softened

3/4 cup sugar, divided	1 teaspoon vanilla
3 eggs (can substitute 2 egg whiles for 1 egg)	1 cup canned pumpkin
3/4 teaspoon cinnamon	1/4 teaspoon ground nutmeg

Combine cream cheese, 1/2 cup sugar, and vanilla in mixing bowl and beat on medium speed until well-blended. Add eggs one at a time, mixing well after each addition. Reserve 1 cup batter. To remaining batter, add 1/4 cup sugar, pumpkin and spices. Alternately layer pumpkin and cream cheese batters over crust. Cut through for a marbled effect. Bake at 350° for 55 minutes. Cool before removing rim of springform pan. Serve chilled.

Giving Thanks

If one characteristic should mark a Christian, it is thankfulness. A Christian is not just gracious and polite. Christians are truly thankful during the ups and downs of life. When the neighbors take another family vacation to Maui, while we can only afford a day at the local water park, we may be tempted to feel sorry for ourselves. However, there is no room for envy or resentment when we are overflowing with thankfulness. Sometimes families focus so much on what they lack that they begin to overlook other blessings. God wants us to be thankful and content with what we have, not resentful about what we do not have. A thankful family always finds things to be grateful for—it can even become a game. If you look around you right now, can you name ten things for which to be thankful, without even leaving the room? Take a moment to reflect on what you are most thankful for.

Family Time

Sometimes we need to take stock of all the blessings we have. Look around you right now. Take turns having each family member finish the following sentence: "This Thanksgiving, I'm most thankful for

_____."

How can we always be thankful, even during the tough times? Why is it necessary to give God thanks?

Dear Father,

You have brought us together as a family—that alone is reason enough to overflow with thankfulness. When we say the words "thank you," help us to mean it in our hearts. We are truly thankful for each gift You have given us. Amen.

Our Family Traditions

Christmas Eve Dinner

O God, Make the door of this house wide enough to receive all who need human love and fellowship, and a heavenly Father's care; and narrow enough to shut out all envy, pride and hate.

Make its threshold smooth enough to be no stumbling-block to children, nor to straying feet, but rugged enough to turn back the tempter's power:

Make it a gateway to thine eternal kingdom.

Thomas Ken

THE CHRISTMAS CONNECTION

Nanette is the instigator. She began the tradition long ago when our girls were very young, and it has become the hallmark of our Christmas time together. On Christmas Eve you will find all five, puttering about the kitchen, preparing for the day to come. Cookies, muffins, and tomorrow's meals are only part of the fare. Their favorite part is the birthday cake.

Come Christmas, we celebrate Jesus' birth—in the most literal way we know how. We light candles on the cake made just for Him, and together we sing "Happy Birthday!" to our Savior. Then, as with all good birthday parties, we eat the cake and open presents, rejoicing in the fun and fellowship our faithful Lord provides. It's a simple but profound way we as a family remember the reality of Jesus' incredible life: that there truly was a time in history when He set aside His royal robes and came to earth as a tiny baby, born to serve. While it warms our hearts, we have to realize that not only is the story of His birth true, but His life, death, and resurrection, as well.

That's why it is so important to share the light of Christmas with others. Yes, it is fun to gather close with family, and certainly right to do so. But by letting others into your home and lives to experience the warmth that comes from Christ, you are actively participating in the real reason for the season. Just like the shepherds and wise men who showed up unannounced to see the Savior, others around you may also be in desperate need of encountering Christ as He manifests Himself in your home or through your family.

Welsh Rarebit

2 tablespoons butter	1 egg yolk, beaten
3 teaspoons flour	1/4 cup beer
2/3 cup milk	1/2 teaspoon Worcestershire sauce
1 cup (8 ounces) shredded cheddar cheese	pinch cayenne pepper
pinch dry mustard	

Place butter in bowl and cook on high in microwave one minute. Stir in the flour and cook on high one minute. Blend in the milk, and cook on high 1-1/2 minutes, stirring twice during cooking. Add shredded cheese, and cook on medium for 4-5 minutes to melt, stirring twice during the cooking. Whisk egg yolk quickly into the cheese sauce. Place beer into a small jug or bowl. Cook on high until reduced to 2 teaspoons. Add to cheese mixture with the seasonings. Keep warm in a fondue pot, and serve with buttered Italian or French bread. Another option is to serve with fresh, cut-up vegetables.

Other Fondue Suggestions

Heat oil or broth in a fondue pot. Dip and cook chicken or beef in it.

7-Layer Salad

1 head lettuce torn into bite-sized pieces

1/2 head cauliflower, chopped

1 (10 ounces) package frozen peas, thawed

1 cup celery, chopped

1/2 cup green onions, chopped

1 medium green pepper, chopped

2 cups mayonnaise

1/4 cup sugar

1/2 cup Parmesan cheese

2 tablespoons vinegar

1 cup (4 ounces) shredded cheddar cheese

1 pound bacon, fried crisp, crumbled

Layer salad ingredients in a 13" x 9" pan. (It looks pretty in a glass dish). Stir together the mayonnaise, sugar, Parmesan cheese, and vinegar. Spread over the salad, sealing to edges. Cover with plastic wrap, and refrigerate overnight. Before serving, garnish with shredded cheese and crisp bacon.

Rack of Lamb with Honey Hazelnut Crust

1 cup ground hazelnuts

1 cup fresh bread crumbs

3 tablespoons chopped fresh rosemary

3 racks of lamb, trimmed

3 tablespoons Dijon mustard

Salt and pepper to taste

3 tablespoons honey

Combine the hazelnuts, bread crumbs, and rosemary in a small bowl;
mix well. Arrange the racks of lamb meat side up on shallow
baking sheets. Brush the lamb with mustard, and season with salt
and pepper. Sprinkle the hazelnut mixture evenly over each rack of lamb.
Drizzle with honey. Roast at 425 degrees for 25 minutes or until done to taste.
Chill, tightly covered, until ready to serve. Yield: 3 to 6 servings

Adapted from a recipe found on Recipezaar.com

Chocolate Chip Pie

2 eggs

1/2 cup flour

1/2 cup sugar

1/2 cup brown sugar

1/2 teaspoon vanilla

1 cup butter, melted and cooled to room temperature

1 cup chocolate chips

1 cup chopped walnuts or pecans

9" unbaked pie shell

optional whipped cream or ice cream

Preheat oven to 325°. In large bowl, beat eggs until foamy; beat in flour, sugar, brown sugar, and vanilla until well blended. Blend in melted butter. Stir in chocolate chips and nuts. Pour into pie shell. Bake at 325° for 1 hour. Remove from oven. Serve warm with whipped cream or ice cream.

Seeing is Believing

Christmas happens more than once a year. It happens each time we experience Jesus firsthand. Christmas is about God's coming into the world in the form of a child, Jesus Christ. However, Christmas remains only a distant story or family tradition until we truly embrace Jesus. The moment we do, we realize that Christmas is about God in the flesh. Christmas happens when we see, experience and share Jesus with those around us—when we share our gifts with a needy child, when we deliver food to a homeless family, when we invite a lonely older person into our home. We celebrate Christmas every time we truly connect with Christ in prayer, when we sense His presence daily, when we walk with Him obediently. Has the true meaning of Christmas hit home this year? Don't wait another season. Experience God in the flesh this day.

Family Time

How do you see Jesus in the world around you? When was a time that you felt like you experienced Him firsthand?

What is your family doing this Christmas season to help others experience Jesus firsthand? Brainstorm some family activities you could do this month to help others experience Christmas—maybe even for the first time. For example, you could choose to go caroling as a family at a nursing home. You could serve a meal at a homeless shelter downtown. What other ideas can you think of as a family?

Dear Father,

This Christmas, help us to say with John that we have seen You with our own eyes. Help us touch You by touching others who need Your love. Help us experience Christmas this year like never before. Amen.

Artwork by Thomas Kinkade
used in Mealtime Memories

Skater's Pond

A Perfect Red Rose

Home Town Chapel

Julianne's Cottage

Olde Porterfield Tea Room

It Doesn't Get Much Better

The Light of Freedom

Perseverance

Sunset at Riverbend Farm

Beginning of a Pefect Evening 1

Blessings of the Season 1

Christmas Eve